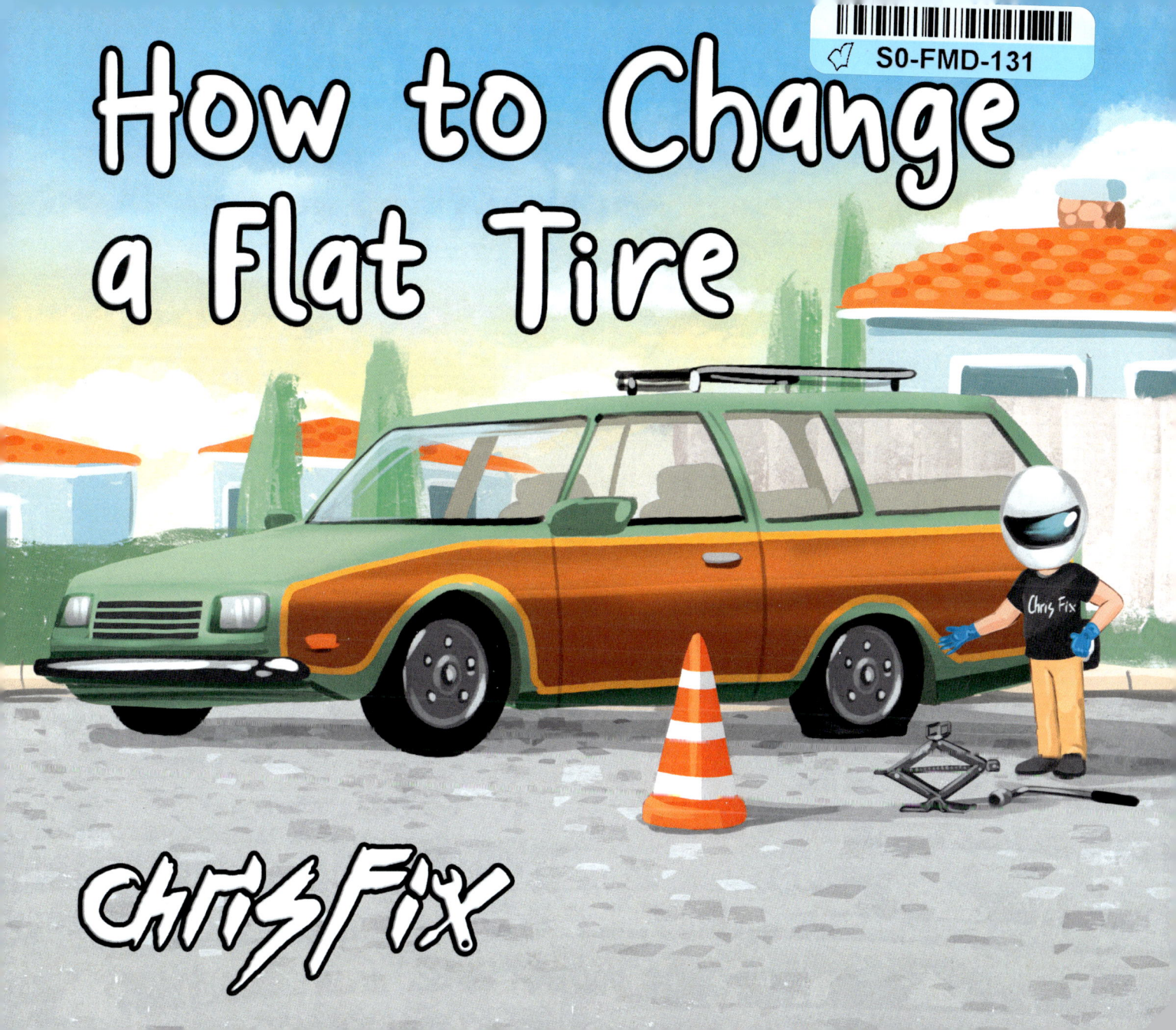

To Mom and Dad, who have always encouraged me to learn and try new things. Thank you for your constant love and support, even with ten project cars in the driveway that barely run.

Scan this QR code to access a video read-along with ChrisFix

Copyright © 2022 ChrisFix LLC. All rights reserved. No part of this book may be reproduced or transmitted in any form or by any means, electronic or mechanical, without written permission from the publisher.
ISBN: 979-8-218-11543-2

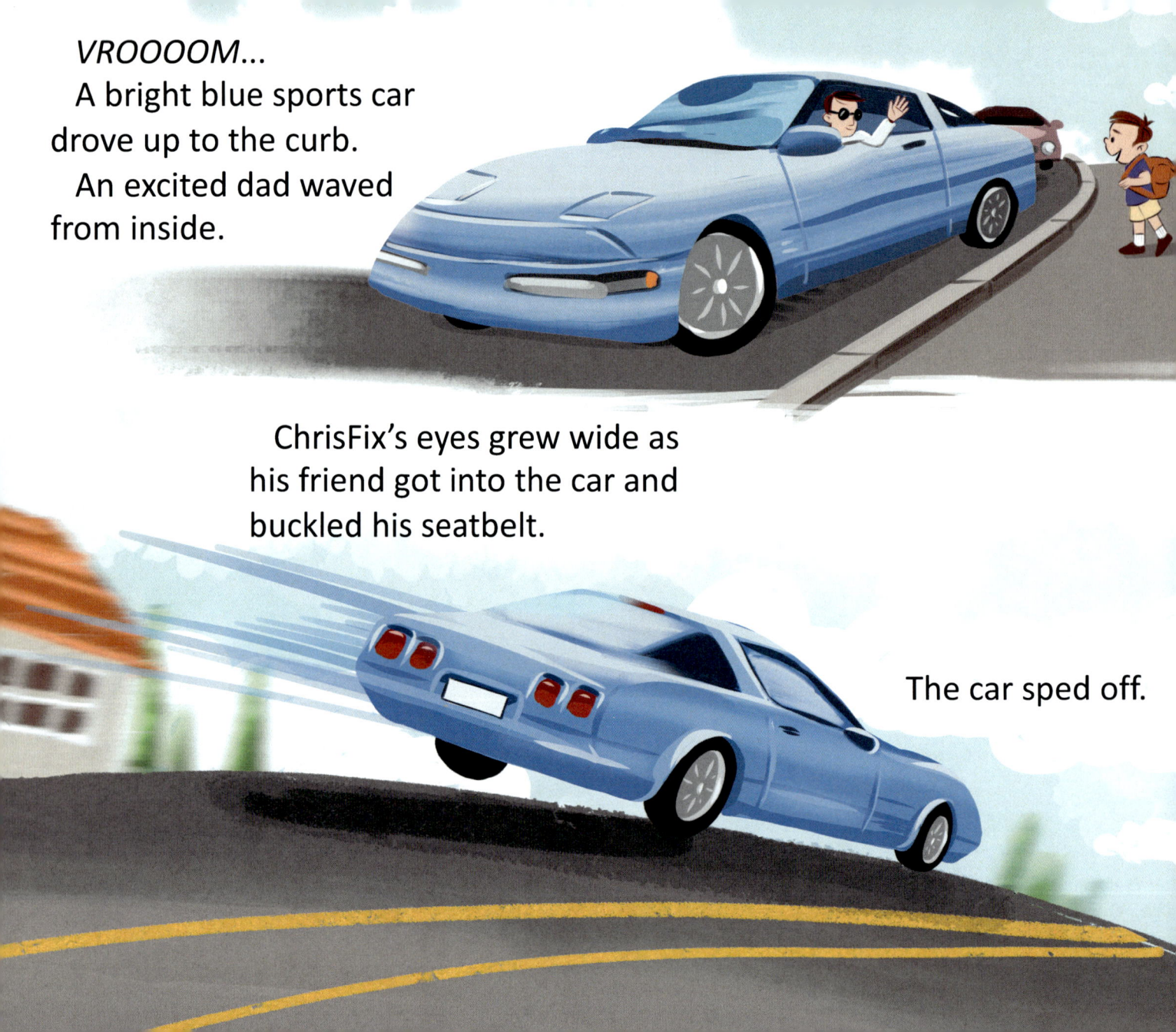

BEEP BEEP!
Susie's family pulled up in front of ChrisFix and his sister in a green woody station wagon.

Susie shut the door behind her. ChrisFix giggled as he saw his weirdly-shaped reflection in the car's paint.

Just then, the eight-year-old heard two familiar voices.
"Hey!" ChrisFix's mom called out from the tan van approaching the sidewalk.
"Are you both ready to go?" ChrisFix's dad added.

The brother and sister nodded and hopped into the van onto the soft, bouncy seats, eager to head home.

The family drove away from the school. ChrisFix was looking out the window when he noticed something strange.

"Oh no!" ChrisFix gasped as the van pulled up to a stop sign. "That's Susie's car, and it has a flat tire! She's on her way to her soccer game. Can we go help?"

"Of course we can!" His dad replied in excitement. "Let's move to the side of the road safely."

ChrisFix's dad parked behind the station wagon, turned on his flashers, and put out emergency cones to alert other drivers.

"I'll be right out, Dad!" ChrisFix yelled. He turned to his sister for help with his backpack. *Ziiiiiip*!

ChrisFix pulled out two blue gloves, stretched out his fingers, and put on his gloves.

Then, he stuck his arm into his backpack and pulled out his shiny, white helmet.

"You've got this!" ChrisFix's mom assured him as he put on his helmet and jumped onto the sidewalk.

"Oh, great timing," Susie said as she hopped out of the car onto the sidewalk. "My soccer tournament is tonight, but we can't get there with a flat tire. Let's get to work!"

With the help of Susie's parents, ChrisFix opened the trunk of the car. He picked up the carpet and removed the spare tire and tools.

"See? Everything we need is right here! We have a lug wrench, a jack, and a spare tire," ChrisFix said.

Chris stood next to the flat tire, put the lug wrench on the lug nut, and tried loosening the first nut with aaaaall his might.

"Hmmm. This is a little tight. Maybe if I...just...jump..." ChrisFix said, breathing heavily from all his hard work.

And just like that, one lug nut was loosened, and Chris was able to loosen the remaining four lug nuts at rapid speed!

"Now, it is time for the jack, which is like an elevator for the car! It is *very* important that you jack up a car safely."

"First, you want to make sure the car is on flat ground."

"Second, pull up the parking brake, so the car doesn't roll."

"Finally, look for notches under the car next to the flat tire. The notches show where the jack should go. Put the jack between the notches."

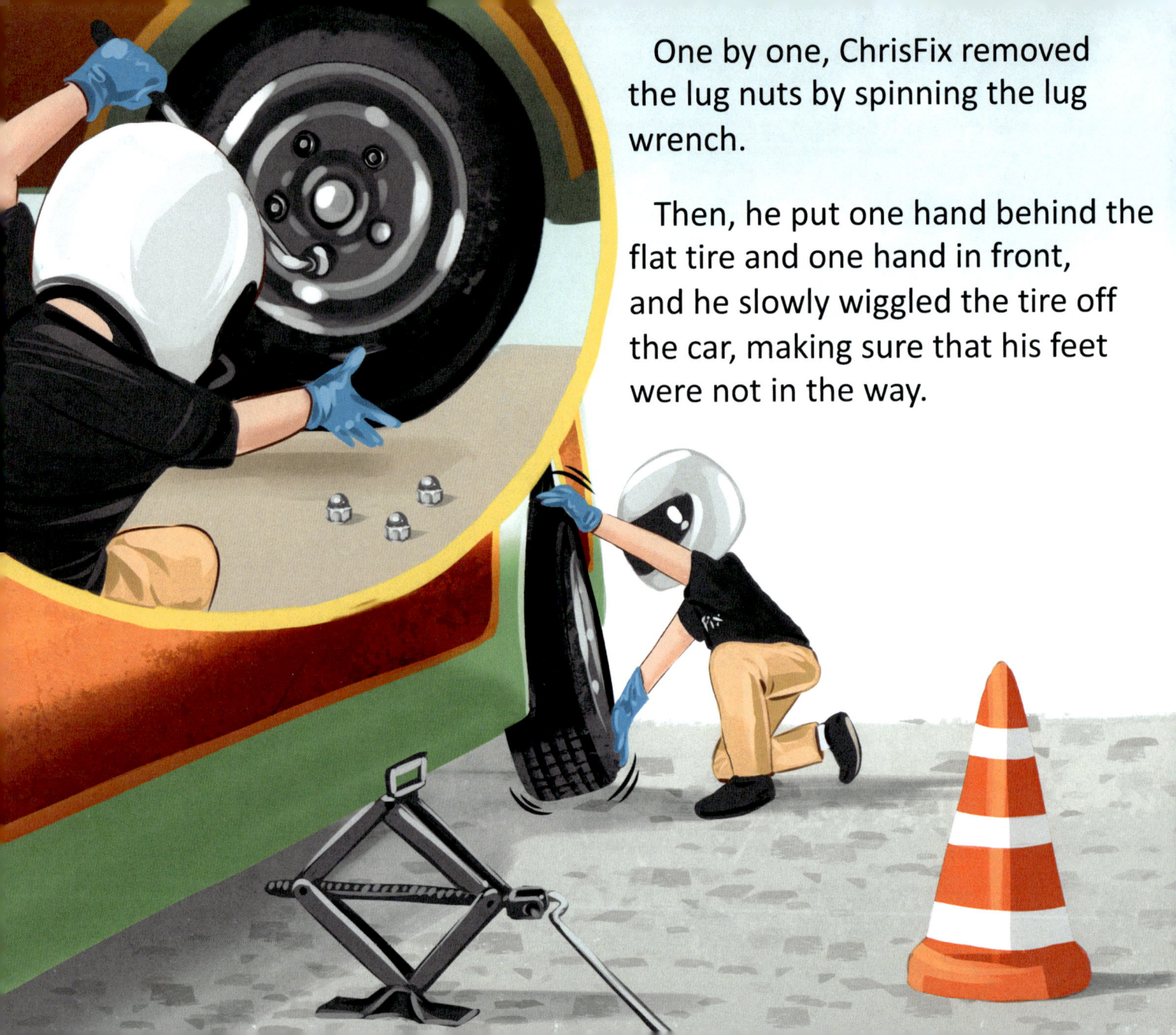

With his dad's help, ChrisFix wiggled the spare tire onto the hub.

"Just a few more minutes, Susie, and you'll be headed to your game!" ChrisFix said. "Can you hand me the lug nuts so I can put them on?"

Susie jumped up to help ChrisFix. One by one, he tightened each lug by hand.

They were ready to move on to the final step!

With a thumbs up from everyone in the van, ChrisFix removed his helmet, jumped into the back seat, and was on his way to the game.

They drove down a long highway with red trucks and yellow buses and finally arrived at the big, green field.

ChrisFix's dad parked the car, and they walked to the bleachers.

Susie's team and the opposing team dribbled up and down the field. The game was close; the score was tied one to one.

ChrisFix
Tire Change Tool Kit

Safely cut out page and add to tool box for reference list of tools needed to change tire. Collect new tools with every book.

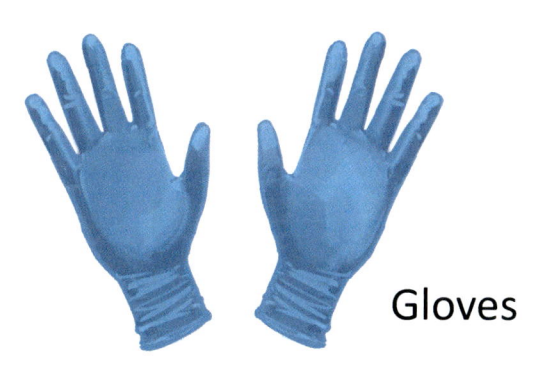
Gloves

Cones

Lug Wrench

Spare Tire

Jack

Made in the USA
Middletown, DE
16 December 2022